Because I Wanted You to Know

Kelly Paragone

To the boys I've loved so far

~

I've been reading a lot of poetry lately

writing a lot of poetry too

do you want to read some of it

quite a few are about you

~

If I lay my truth at your feet

will you accept it

will you invite it in

for tea

& a nice chat

will you let it hang out

on your porch

but close the blinds

& pretend it isn't there

or will you lock the door

& turn out the lights

no one's home

sorry

not sorry

~

I spent 23 years

Carefully building the walls around my heart

Brick by brick

With meticulous precision

And you're telling me

I'm supposed to tear it down

In the face of love

& let my bleached heart burn

Ha

Don't expect me to reverse

A lifetime of work

In one year

One relationship

Love has made me soft

But it has not made me

Less afraid

I will slam those gates shut

If you so much as

Laugh in the wrong direction

The walls did nothing to protect me

Instead

They made me fragile

       Without resilience

The walls are coming down

Brick by brick

With meticulous precision

The work of a lifetime

Give me time

To acclimate my tender heart

The climate is harsh

& it hurts

To look directly at the sun

~

How the fuck is anyone vulnerable

when the chance of getting hurt is so high

How am I supposed to believe in my right to exist

when I've been shamed so many times

I'm choking on the indecision

The desire to be seen vs. the desire to be safe

Is there a scenario in which

I can breathe easy

~

I'm a gen z bitch

raised on

Taylor Swift lyrics

& YA books

that made boys

seem like gentle creatures

I'm nostalgic

& sentimental

& sensitive

& all the things

I shouldn't be

to survive in this world

I don't believe that what I have to say

matters

but I'm trying

I'm not exactly the next poet laureate

but I wrote these poems anyway

sharing my words with you

is the hardest thing I'll ever do

but I'm doing it anyway

~

You were both born

when the sun was in Cancer

Almost exactly

a year apart

One of you loves to use

your crab claws to pinch

The other is stuck

in your shell

I love you Cancer boys

in all your crab glory

Because the water runs deep

within you

& I love swimming in the depths

of your soul

~

My heart broke

(the first time)

in the car with Amy

delivering valentines on a February day

I didn't know heartbreak was so literal

     heart   break

I pressed my fingers to my aching chest

felt my sternum & the ribs beneath my breasts

skinnier than before

I hadn't noticed I was losing weight

I'm just a cliché now

fuck

~

Why do I want him

But not

Don't want to date him

But don't want him to date other girls either

Don't want to fuck him

But want him to want to fuck me

~

My back hurts from bending over to blow you

my thighs are sore from straddling

does your body feel the residual fallout of our mistake

like mine does

we said we don't regret it

are we both lying?

you said there's no more emotional connection

why is that such a punch to the gut

when I feel the same way

don't say it out loud

we're a perfect fit

you said so yourself

(once upon a time)

you don't like that I'm bolder

what I really mean is *louder*

you never liked my moans

said it felt fake

so I was the quiet girl you wanted

well, guess what

I found someone who likes my vocal expression

he thinks it's hot

he makes me *feel* hot

a concept that was hard for you to grasp

so self assured you were

but I needed help

(I wish you could've been the one)

I don't want to feel guilty for growing

for fucking a man who talks dirty

who isn't silent with his pleasure

who doesn't silence me

I didn't know I needed that

until I found it

with him

~

Let it go or let me go

that's what I said

but not what I meant

please don't let me go

I mean more to you

than one mistake

please

let it go

trust me

it's so easy

forgiveness is easy

when compassion abounds

~

Don't you know
I feel safe with you
I don't feel that way with just anyone

I showed you my toe socks
& my sheep sweater
my body
& my brain

We still weren't right for each other

Was it because I brought a book to your softball game
        because I didn't listen the way you needed me to
        because I didn't want to drive on the turnpike late
        at night
        (even though that was the best time to drive it)

Was I awakening
or was I drowning
Hard to tell from this angle
Could be both

Was definitely both

Why did it have to be both

~

You used me

I was a vessel to empty yourself into

Yeah

I let you do it

even though you were the one who told me I'm worth

more than that

Were you lying to me

or are you just the exception

to all my rules

You said I'm easy

then later

told me there was no connection

You are a dick

But I would say yes to you again

so I guess that makes me a slut

~

you said it was a new beginning

a new era

you said you were excited

EXCITED!

I remember your smile

as I said goodbye

that day

I really believed you

when you said

this was a new beginning

then you blocked my number

???

what am I missing

well, I'm missing you

but that's a stupid joke

what I'm missing is

your perspective

your thoughts

your presence

Laura says I have to be patient
my tarot cards tell me the same thing
patience is a bitch
who I want to punch
in the face

it's so hard
because
you said

it was a new beginning
(& I believed you)
but what you really meant was
this is just another ending

~

you think you're mature
but you're just insecure
you're bouncing around
without purpose
without love & empathy
for yourself
stop blaming everyone else
for once in your life
shut the fuck up
& LISTEN

~

How fucking dare you

Put your body into mine

& ask me to compare the two of you

We both know you won't like the answer

I never give you the right answer

(The answer you want to hear)

But I still want to please you

I'd do anything to please you

Why can't I please you

How fucking dare you

Put your body into mine

& tell me after

That there was no emotional connection

Anymore

I offered myself up to you on a silver platter

(like a fucking idiot)

& you complained about the meal

After licking the plate clean

How fucking dare you

Put your body into mine

& use our time together

To talk about him

Why can't it be enough

That I'm here

You called &

I came

(like a fucking idiot)

I gave you everything you wanted

It still wasn't enough

Why am I never enough

~

You want an explanation

that's not there

I didn't mean to hurt you

I was naïve

I was stupid

I was confused

Those aren't excuses

They're the truth

Sometimes people just make mistakes

I made a mistake

You say that downplays what happened

It doesn't

You are shattered

That's ok

You are allowed to feel

anything & everything

Your pain needs no validation correlation

Because you feel them

they are valid

You want me to admit I did it on purpose

so you can feel better about hating me

but that's not how this works

~

You blocked me

again

you leave &

you come back

it's the cycle of life

it's the cycle of our life

have you ever noticed

that I never leave

why do you get to be the one

with all the power

you give

you take away

& I feel crushed

every

single

time

did you know that?

did you know that your actions

crush me

it's so hard to comfort you

when you're hurting me

I guess I could leave

I could walk away

because I don't deserve to be treated

this way

but I don't

I will always be waiting

for you

to come back

please come back

~

Will I see you in a year?

a year

a year

a year

isn't that long

in the grand scheme of things

except

I can barely get through

Aries season

without reaching out

reaching out…

such a beautiful phrase

makes me think of

The Creation of Adam

on the ceiling of the Sistine Chapel

to reach

to reach out

to reach toward

to reach toward *you*

I'm always reaching toward you

how long must I wait

before we finally

touch

Voice memo #9

Hey…I know you asked for space, but I really want to talk to you. I'm not going to send this, but I need to say some things, and this way I can at least pretend I'm talking to you. How pathetic is that? What's even more pathetic is that I don't even care. So, uh, I miss you. Fuck. I didn't think I would start crying so soon. I'm sorry. I've been crying a lot lately. I miss you so much and it hurts a lot. I'm not doing well. I don't know why I said that. That's not what I wanted to tell you. I wanted to tell you that I miss your friendship. I know we can't get back together and that's ok. I'm really ok with that. I'm just so lonely. I greatly underestimated how lonely I was & now that you're gone the emptiness is so much heavier than I remembered from before.

I know it's not your responsibility to keep me afloat. It never was, even if I sometimes let you take on that role. I'm sorry. I shouldn't have done that. I'm different now. I'm growing. I see everything so much clearer now. I know what I need to do. I just want you in my life. You know me better than anyone. I trust you. I need you.

I know you asked for space, but it's killing me. When will you come back to me?

Will you please come back…?

~

You were upset that a text from him

lifted my sour mood

from winter blue to giddy yellow

yeah, well

a text from you does the same thing

a text from anybody who gives a shit about me

lifts my mood

I'm lonely & desperate for validation

I thought you knew that

~

Look at you
jumping to conclusions

leap

leap

leap

Chani says we jump to conclusions to escape
something that is uncomfortable for us
I'm uncomfortable for you
I hurt you
stop trying to escape
stop blocking my number
every time you miss you
every time you're angry
about the things you can't control
stop running
stop
leaping
turn around
& face me

face yourself

the most uncomfortable thing of all

~

I don't know why you're so mad at me

for dating a boy who is nice to me

he's using me for sex?

so what

I'm using him for sex too

he's bad at communication?

yeah, same

I just don't understand

why it sets you off

so explosively

you don't just disagree with my choices

you HATE me for them

you fly off the fucking handle

every time you bring him up

I don't understand!

I want to understand

are you jealous?

you should be

although, I should say

you're not winning any points by

treating me like shit

you're driving me into his arms

when all I want

is to be wrapped up

by you

~

Why did we even break up

in the first place

that October day

over the phone

I was at work

picking apples

my phone zipped up

in the bib pocket

of my overalls

I hadn't seen you in two weeks

we were fighting a lot

but not about the things that mattered

you said you had a lot going on

but weren't telling me what those things were

I think you wanted me to

make you feel better

but without you having to tell me

what was wrong

that was an impossible ask

that's not how relationships work

that's not how communication works

& when I literally asked you

what you needed from me

you said

if I had to ask

I was an idiot

that was unfair of you

that was me trying to communicate

that I was there for you

but I can't read your mind

I was giving you the opportunity

to be mature

& ask for what you needed

I would have done the best I could

I think it was proof of my growth

that I thought to ask

but you turned it back around

& made me feel stupid

that was one of our worst fights

but I don't know

why we broke up

for all your talk of open communication

you were pretty shitty at

communicating to me

what was going on

the blame is not wholly on you

but that time was so confusing for me

I wonder if you could shed some light

I think we broke up

because we needed room to grow

& we were stifling each other

we wanted different things

we were so frustrated

that we couldn't make each other

into the people we wanted

we loved each other deeply

but had trouble loving each other's

limitations

the ones that kept us from being who we could be

Why did we break up when we did?

how we did?

if we had seen each other

physically

in the same room

& talked

we could have pushed our relationship further

instead of jumping ship

in rough waters

but who knows

maybe not

I was angry at you

for so many things

& I was itching for the world

to open up to me

We broke up for a reason

even if it was confusing

& everything that came after

was fucked

Whatever the reason

(does it matter now)

I'm so grateful

that what happened then

has led me to where

I am now

Interlude #4

I was really in my feels in therapy, so there wasn't much "real work" going on. Sure sure, maybe the real work is feeling my emotions, but that's painful so I don't want to believe it. There was one tangible piece of information that was worth the $160 I spent to cry on someone else's couch. My therapist told me that it's possible to set boundaries about how I will and will not accept being treated.

For example, I can say to D., "I want to support you when you're upset, and I want to be here to listen to you, but if start yelling at me or calling me names, I will leave the conversation."

I mean, wow! What a badass move that would be!

I said to her, "I didn't know you could do that."

She smiled. "Yeah, pretty cool, right?"

I'm such a doormat. Nah. More like a paper towel. I soak up whatever shit comes out of D.'s mouth until I'm limp and dirty. But hey, at least I was useful. I never tell him that his words hurt me because I know he'll get upset if I do.

I don't think that's how it's supposed to be.

Maybe I deserve to be treated better.

I think I I deserve to be treated better.

One more time so I pretend to believe it.

I deserve to be treated better!

~

Why do you enjoy pointing out all my flaws

In fucking high definition

You want me to hurt

You admitted it

You aimed & fired

With intentional precision

I cried & cried

You didn't stop your verbal assault

& I didn't walk away

Intention / Attention

I begged for your forgiveness

Said over & over

How I never intended to hurt you

You said it didn't matter

Doesn't it though?

Doesn't it matter?

You intentionally hurt me

Because I unintentionally hurt you

I think that matters a whole lot

~

You called me a slut

but you're the one who fucked me

~

Why am I protecting you?

I can only feel

      guilty

For so long

You hurt me too, ya know

If I told my mom how you treated me

She would hate me for staying

If I had any self respect

I would hate me for staying too

You always had a reason

An explanation

A display of emotion

I always forgave you

My reasons were never good enough

But why

"But why"

But why

      You always said

I DON'T KNOW

I was scared

I was naïve

I was reckless

Why isn't that good enough

Just because you don't understand

Doesn't mean I was lying

What's the definition of gaslighting?

I think that's what you did to me

But I'll defend you

Till my dying day

Because you're weird

    & dorky

    & kind

I love your giggle

    & your eyes

    & your voice

I love your mom

I love your heart

I love your brain

So I'll lie to myself

To keep you in my life

Because you're worth more to me

Than all my

    guilt

    & shame

    & anger

But you hurt me too, ya know

You hurt me too

~

Names You Called Me

LIAR

SLUT

DUMBASS

PUSHOVER

EMOTIONLESS ROBOT (a personal favorite)

STUPID

TOXIC

Kell

~

I helped you find a therapist

right in time

for you to find another girl

~

The Very Next Day

you went to her

tested me out again

after months apart

didn't like the ride

so you put me away

went out to try the shiny new model

The Very Next Day

~

Did you tell your parents

about February

Did you tell your therapist

I doubt it

You don't want to admit to the people on your side

that you made mistakes

& caused me pain

So you paint me the villain

every time

& turn them all against me

Don't worry

I kill with kindness

~

I broke myself in two
to earn your forgiveness
& you never even said
sorry

~

Shame is
the shadow
swallowing the sun

Shame is
your dream
where the breaks go out

Shame is
the rusty shovel
digging your grave

Shame is
the biggest mistake
of your life

Shame is
every small mistake
you ever made

Shame is
a cold sweat

Shame is
the desire to
turn back time

Shame is
a lonely stage
& a full audience

Shame is
your body
in a cage

Interlude #9

I did a shitty job painting my toenails, but I don't care. I thought I was happy, but maybe I'm sad. I thought I could tell the difference, but maybe I can't. Could it just be boredom? That feeling between happy and sad. Is this the place I lived in all those years before I found a boy who told me I was pretty?

Now I'm sitting in my closet and it's cold because I have the window open. My throat is tight again, like how it always was when I was a kid. It hasn't been tight for a while. That's a sign that things are changing. Changing for the worse maybe.

I don't know how I can eat dinner with my family and not say a single word throughout the whole meal and get away with it. I guess I'm glad that I do get away with it, because I don't want to talk to them. They don't tell me I'm pretty. They don't hug me.

I guess I feel this way because I lost D. again. Even though he's sending me sad reels about true love, I think it's going to work this time.

I think I liked the drama. It's not something that I want to admit about myself, but it's true. Even if we were arguing, even if I wanted to wring his neck, even when he was angry with me, at least there was something going on. It's so quiet now. I like it, but I wonder for how long. How much time do I have before the crippling depression slinks back in? I'm so afraid.

Here's what I want: to meet an aristocratic boy from a wealthy family who will ask me to spend the summer with him in Martha's Vineyard. That's literally it.

If I got that, I might be able to marry D. after all.

When did marriage become a real thing I could think about in the context of my life? Marriage means nothing more to me than slipping on my mom's heels and hobbling my toddler feet down the yoga mat aisle in my sister's game of house. I don't know what it means in real life. There are married couples all around me, but they're not like me. They're adults. I am but a child.

When D. tells me he wants to spend the rest of his life with me, I don't doubt him, but I also want to laugh in his face and say, good joke. He wants stability and structure and he thinks marriage will accomplish that. In theory, yes. But if I've learned anything over the past year it's that love is hard. Like, really hard.

I thought things were always supposed to work out for the characters in stories. Lies! But then again, we're not characters in a story. This is real life.

Or is it…

~

Hold me again

tell me

"I've got you"

You have no idea

how many wounds you've healed

with those three words

~

I hate her
for everything she is
that I could never be

she's better at communicating
she asks about your feelings
she isn't afraid to go to Target
you can cry in front of her
apparently you couldn't do that with me
because I'm such a cold hearted bitch
Right?

Really
I just hate myself
& jealousy
is the only cold hearted bitch
around here

I didn't love you the way you wanted me to
& she does
at least

you want her to

until she does something you don't like

& you tear her apart

like you did to me

again & again

I sat there

& took it

I hope she never does

I hope she's stronger than me

then I'll respect her

for everything she is

that I could never be

~

You're "therapist approved"

cool

wait till you break her heart

then her therapist won't be so approving

my therapist liked you too

until

well…

until you

shot me down

& kicked me while I bled out

Maybe all three of our therapists

should get together

maybe they could

solve all our problems for us

it'd be a hell of a good time

~

I want to gossip about you
to someone who will understand

What's her number
I'm sure we'd get along great

Jerked Around: A Journey

Jerk me around, why don't ya

send me mixed signals

block my number

then call me late at night

 If hope is the thing with feathers

you shot that bitch out of the sky

& plucked each feather

one by one

with malicious satisfaction

        wait

        I'm doing it again

        casual sarcasm to avoid emotions

        pause

        reassess

vulnerability is brave

vulnerability is brave

(can you tell I'm trying to convince myself)

let's talk about our feelings

Yay!!

goddammit

I did it again

*shaky breath

ok

I cry in my closet

every time you shoot me down

even though you were the one

who encouraged me to fly

I choke on my sobs

every time you come back

just to make sure I still miss you

I pick myself up

every time you (predictably)

depart again

once I've satisfied your sadistic need

to witness my pain

one day at a time

until I'm okay

(but not fine)

until you come back around

again

& it feels so good

it feels like a nice hug on a rough day

then you become my rough day

I don't want you to stop

but I want you to know

    I've died

     & been reborn

     countless times

in the cycle of your indecision

you're not the only one coming to the phone

a new version every time

I have feelings too

I have feelings!

I feel sad

I feel angry

I feel undervalued

I feel raw

I feel small

I feel stupid

I feel unseen

I feel unheard

I feel wounded

I feel lost

I feel alone

I feel love

      just a reminder

I'm not telling you this

because I'm looking for something

from you

I'm telling you this

because my feelings are important

I don't have to be silent

anymore

~

Can I be internal and external at the same time?

Can I only write in this state of peril?

But can I *live* in this state of peril?

Which is more important to me?

~

Our fights were so stupid

you got made because

I didn't care about the construction

in your town

you got mad when

I pointed out that

you put the dog crate

in your room

even though

Forrest can't go up the stairs

you got mad because

I was nervous

at the flower farm

you got mad because

you swore you told me

you were visiting your friend at Penn State

(you never told me)

look at this list

take a good long look

why the fuck did we fight

you need to calm down

seriously

are you ok bro

~

You don't like that you still love me

because you have a girlfriend

& she's not me

I know you

I know your brain

you feel guilty for

thinking about me

when you're with her

I wish you weren't so hard

on yourself

I wish you weren't so hard

on me either

I really miss you calling me

killer

~

An ode

to my

earthy hand job

an apt name

for me on you

fingers warm

from me to you

~

I live to make you laugh

to see you hunch your shoulders

& cover your mouth

as if to hide your joy

I want you to look at me like you love me

isn't laughter love?

please, let it be love

I have nothing else to offer

but my dry humor

& sarcastic comments

but please

laugh

because

when you laugh

I love you back

Interlude #8

D.'s having a hard time. He hasn't been eating or sleeping and doesn't want to be alone with his own brain. I offered him my bed to sleep in. That was the wrong thing to say. Why do I always say the wrong thing?

I know that I am the comfort he craves the most. It's a responsibility I take seriously. A power wielded with mindfulness and respect. At least, I try to achieve as much. I know sometimes I'm clumsy and hurtful.

Like offering my bed, without me in it. My best attempt at giving him the safety he needs becomes tainted because of the status of our relationship. But the status of our relationship is that he's my best friend and I would offer up anything to ease his pain.

The rules and regulations of relationships is confusing to me and I don't understand why we can't just love different people in different ways at the same time.

I love D. here and now. I feel the burden of his pain. I wish to make him feel better. I have the power to help him, so why shouldn't I exercise that power to the best of my ability.

Love is more complicated than I thought, but sometimes it's very simple.

~

If I don't feel pain
I don't feel you
and I want you
right here

~

I feel lightheaded

with hope

every time

my phone chirps

because

my body thinks

it's a message from you

I wish my body

would catch up

to my broken heart

because

I feel lightheaded

with hope

but it's never

you

~

Your new girlfriend looks like me

if I waxed my eyebrows

& had a less magnetic smile

    I'm sorry

    Was that too mean?

What if I said

I want to rip her heart out

& shove it down her throat

so she chokes on her own blood

    Too much??

    Or just enough

~

I want to be friends with her

not to keep my enemies closer

but because I love you

& I want to love the people you love

I have so much love to give

I really do!

I didn't realize before

how deep the well was

I didn't even know there was a well!

but there it is

in the deep pit

of my heart

a deep reserve

I've learned to tap

Don't be suspicious

I'm not scheming to get you back

I don't want to go that way

that girl was cold & afraid

in the twilit woods of love

without a map or a candle to guide her

I'm not afraid anymore
I'm not afraid to say
I LOVE YOU!
& I love her too

Do you believe me?

Can you let me back in
so I can show you

Memories: #1

we were naked

on the couch

I was on top

you said "are you okay?"

did I look sad

or something

how did you know

to ask that

I said "yeah"

I lied

we kept going

I didn't want to stop

again, you said

"are you okay?"

I burst into tears

we were naked

on the couch

talking

I said "I'm sorry I didn't let you finish"

you said "this was so much better"

~

I find reasons to say your name

so I don't forget how it feels in my mouth

~

Do you think about me

When she's between your legs

I bet I give a better blowjob

I bet you agree

Even if you won't admit it

I'm a 10/10 baby

Everyone says so

Do you miss the way I squirm under your touch

Do you miss the way I taste

                the way I sound

Do you miss my tight little pussy

Yeah

I bet you do

It could all be yours again

For the low, low price

Of basic human empathy

~

I'm so unreasonable

Unhinged

Remember when you—

[redacted]

[redacted]

[redacted]

I won't embarrass you

But we both know what you did

And *I'm* the unhinged one

Ok

You're allowed to be hysterical

But I'm not

I comforted you

Every time

I forgave you

Immediately

For every psychotic thing you did

I talked you down

When you were crying on the phone

I forgave you

It was easy

Forgiveness is easy

with a little bit of empathy

(the thing you said I lack)

EMPATHY: the ability to understand and share the

feelings of others

(according to Google)

Kinda feels like the thing

you lack

Don't ya think

I have too much empathy

Otherwise

How could I still love you

after every unhinged thing you did

I'll tell you how I did it

Listen close

I put myself in your shoes

I felt your fear

I felt your love

I felt your desperation
I felt your anger

Love is easy
when you see humans as human
Love is easy
with a little bit of empathy

Do you think you could try
to have some empathy?
For me?

Please?

~

I think about you & her

        you *with* her

        (in the biblical sense)

all the time

am I sick

for being

excited

by the thought

can I watch you

can I study you

the way you move

from the outside

I'd keep my eyes wide open

this time

I bet she's pretty naked

I want to follow the curve of her hips

with my eyes

I want to trace your fingers on her back

like soft velvet

does she wrap her legs around you

& pull you deeper

does she take you all

& still want more

god

I want you so bad

when you're fucking someone else

~

I'm keeping my hands busy
to distract my mind
from thoughts of you

I need to stock up on craft kits
it's gonna be a long year

Memories: #4

your

cum

came

out my nose

we laughed

& laughed

~

I was so worried about late nights

& early mornings

I get headaches

you know

when I don't get enough sleep

you lived so far away

our work schedules

never lined up

but I came to you

sweaty and covered in dust

right from work

during the summer months

I tried

for you

I wanted to spend

all my time

with you

I wish I had done more

(why didn't you do more)

I didn't know love was more important

than the price of gas

~

I couldn't love you

enough

until it was

too late

~

I'm not careful

with boy's hearts

I would never have described myself as

reckless

I've never been

reckless

in my life

but you pointed it out to me

& now I can't stop thinking about it

I hate

fucking up

shame

eats at me

from the sternum out

I didn't know

I didn't even know

I was reckless

until I broke your heart

little by little

I hate myself

for what I did

even when

I don't even know

what I did

I wonder if

I'm a bad person

I must be

because

I didn't even know

I was reckless

I want you to know

I didn't mean it

I really didn't mean it

I don't want to be

that girl

I'm sorry that I was

more sorry than you

will ever know

~

Why are you so afraid

to listen

to what I have to say

you beg me to talk

but you never listen

your mind is made up

before I even open my mouth

so what's the point

why pretend to care

when you clearly don't

Interlude #3

I took a bath yesterday and spent the whole time sobbing. One of those *what am I doing with my life* moments. My ex-boyfriend turned (eventual) best friend hates me because I started dating someone else. I can't believe I hurt him so bad. I was so stupid thinking that we were on the same page about things. How could I have treated him like a lover, all the while knowing that I had no intention to get back together with him. I assumed he felt the same way, but I was wrong.

And then O. texted me back after three weeks away and I jumped at the chance to see him. In D.'s eyes, I betrayed him. I was so cavalier. I was so ignorant to D.'s feelings.

Then he sends me some unhinged texts and I call him crying because he said he didn't want to talk to me anymore. He tells me that O. is going to hurt me so bad I'm going to be "obliterated" and he doesn't want to stick around to watch that happen. I stand in the cold barn, hiding from my boss, tears streaming down my face, and let him say horrible things to me.

Why can he never see when he's hurting me?

Why do I let him get away with it?

So I say, okay, okay, okay. Let me make some mistakes. And he says, I need to take some time away. And it crushes me. But I understand. Then he cries and we're telling each other how much we love each other. I make him laugh by saying how pathetic we are. Two hopelessly sad kids, hurting each other over and over, yet bonded by our love.

There's a freedom in space. Possibility.

Then, the claustrophobic truth that life is everchanging. I didn't sign up for that. I want to gain, gain, gain. Gain people who teach me about new parts of myself. Gain experiences I can value forever. Gain hugs and cuddles. I can't bear the feeling of loss. If I had known that this is what life was like, I would've stayed sheltered and pining.

Possibility loses its shiny luster.

I'd rather live in my head than in my flesh. I end up crying in the pink water of my bath.

Then I try to keep things light and hook up with O. in the very casual way of two guarded people who want connection but won't let the other person in. And it's fun and I feel silly. I never feel silly. O. tells me I'm beautiful and I have a nice butt. He squeezes my knee and I laugh uncontrollably and he tells me he likes my toothy grin. No one's ever told me I have a toothy grin before. I like it. I like him. I like that he likes me.

I'm secretly glad I'm not D.'s girlfriend anymore. I will be here until the end of time for him, but he needs to build himself back up.

My responsibility is contained within the boundaries of friendship. If those boundaries are enforced.

The voice in my head loves to hype me up with backhanded shame.

You're strong enough to shoulder the weight. You can hold your own struggles, and the heft of D.'s mental health, and then hide it all with O. and pretend to be a kind and generous girl who will listen to his problems and give him blowjobs.

Yeah, you're strong enough. Your eyes are swollen and heavy from crying, but it's no one's problem but your own.

~

I'm so ashamed of how I treated you

December / February

We talk about December

over & over

We talk about February

never ever

I played with your heart

then you played with mine

You won't shut up about December

but I never talk about February

Funny

isn't it

December

we were getting close again

working weekends at the farm

selling Christmas trees & Christmas cheer

huddled in the shed

you were flirting with girls

on dating apps

& I was flirting with him

at least, until he went away

(a poem for another day)

we had the best sex

we've ever had

that day I came over

with my notes & my naïve enthusiasm

determined to find you a therapist

& stitch together the pieces

of your patchwork heart

I left you in the afternoon

loving you more than I ever had before

it was a really great day

wasn't it?

we were friends

in such a beautiful way

then

Wednesday after Christmas

family dinner

sad sex

you hugged me on the porch

in the cold

when it was all too much

two days later

he texted me

oh, hey!

(I knew you'd come back)

two days after that

I was in his bed

it's true

I didn't know how much that hurt you

until after the fact

until all these months later

you still can't get past it

I said, "I don't understand what I did

to make you hate me"

you said, "you slept with another guy"

Yeah

I did

but we weren't together anymore

broken   up

I did not cheat on you

(louder for the people in the back)

I DID NOT CHEAT ON YOU

I made a choice

that I don't regret

my only regret

is how I handled you

I never meant to hurt you

We were broken up

for a reason

I thought you didn't want me anymore

but I still wanted you

(I didn't want to let go)

& that scared me

I was confused

Clearly, so were you

I'm responsible for my choices

(all the things I did & didn't say)

But you're responsible too

You could have said something

You could have shared your feelings

You could have asked to try again

before it was too late

     You chose not to

Why can't you admit what a

major miscommunication

it was

that's all it was

Misunderstanding

I was lost

I was protecting myself

from being hurt by you again

Ironic

Since I hurt you worse

& fucked my chances to be with you forever

I didn't know how to have a relationship with you

without *being* in a relationship with you

We didn't have the tools to fix what was broken

We didn't even try

We put a pretty little bandage over everything

but never inspected the wound

He was my way out

without having to tell you

I wanted out

I wanted out of the way things were

Now we'll never know the way

of what could have been

<u>February</u>

things had settled into a chilly friendship

checking in & taking care

you were starting something real with her

& I had a thing with him

(complicated but simple all the same)

she wasn't giving you her body

& I was your second choice

ha

(the parallels are too good to be true)

I'm an easy yes

no self respect

when I asked if this would count

as you cheating on her

you said, "I don't know"

(what was I thinking)

when I came over

you sat me down on the opposite couch

& talked as if you were interrogating me

or maybe interviewing me

for the job ahead

I should've known

it didn't feel right

but I passed the test

& I said yes

I wanted it to be like it was

it wasn't

you were kind of mean

but when I cried

you wiped my tears

& that was really sweet

you know I always forgive you

until you said

"that was really great, but

there's no emotional connection between us

anymore"

then you went to her

the very next day!

by the weekend

you were her boyfriend

all you had to say for yourself was

"I'm sorry it hurt you,

but I meant what I said"

then never brought it up again

you crumpled me like a piece of trash

& expected me to move on

even as

my body was still warm from your kisses

You will hate me until the end of time

for what I did

Yet you can't seem to face

the facts

You did the exact same thing to me that I did to you

Fucking poetic justice

How does it feel to have conflicting feelings?

You didn't mean to hurt me

Yeah

Sounds familiar

Like the last time I cried in your bed

I'm sad

that we can never go back

& be as pure

as when we first met

Sometimes I think

it had to happen the way it did

Nothing is by accident

Don't you think?

Our breakup was a six month expedition

through uncharted territory

where we kept learning the same lesson

over & over

& that's no accident

December happened

but so did February

Please don't forget that

It's proof that

you know how I feel

& I know how you feel

There's no reason to pretend otherwise

You are my mirror image

& I am yours

Look at me

        &

           SEE

~

When you fell asleep
I whispered in your ear
"I love you so much"
I don't think you heard me
so I'm telling you now

Intrusive Thought #2

If I can't have him

I should just let any guy

do whatever they want

to me

it doesn't matter

I don't matter

Voice of Reason

Girl

That's the stupidest shit

I ever heard

~

I never cry while making love to him

But I always do with you

~

What pains me the most
is that you turned your parents
against me
I asked you if they hate me
You didn't deny it

      To your mom—
      if you're reading this
      I'm so sorry
      for hurting your son
      I didn't handle him
      with as much care
      as I should have
      I made a mistake
      I really didn't mean to
      I'm glad he had you
      in the aftermath
      I kind of wish
      I had you too
      Please
      Even if we never speak again
      I need you to know

I'm sorry &

I'm going to spend my life

not only working to earn

his forgiveness

but yours as well

P.S. Thank you

for welcoming me

into your home

& into your family

You're warmth & kindness

was the cherry on top of

the most exciting year of my life

spent in your home

with your son

Thank you

~

I know I've hit a low point

when the billboards on the turnpike

make me nostalgic

Memories: #7

we went to Rita's

with your mom

I got cherry water ice

sat in the backseat

my teeth turned red

wearing borrowed socks & Birks

summer nights

& summer fights

it was so nice

to be a part

of your family

~

You broke my heart

but I would still give you

the shattered pieces

cradled in my hands

an offering

kill me again

or kiss the pieces back together

A Dream I Had

I looked at you

across the nose

of our sweet child

& I mouthed

     I love you

And your moonlit eyes whispered back

     I love you more

And our child—the flesh and blood

of our love

Slept warmly in the space

between us

Through Your Window

I watched the seasons change
From the safety of your bed
In the warmth of your body
& the light of your love

We met when the trees were bare
& the air was cold
I watched the branches sway in dusky light
Through your window

You said you loved me when the cherry blossoms
bloomed
& the sky turned blue
I heard the birds sing sweetly
Through your window

You were my solace in the heat
& endless sweat of summer
I loved the storms & rain I witnessed
Through your window

We started to fight when the leaves browned
& the sun sank early
I watched the colors fade
Through your window

I lost you when the Christmas lights twinkled
& the air was gray with snow

I watched the crows scream at me
"Don't go!"
Through your window

Now
I miss your window
& your bed
& all the things you said

~

We didn't talk for two weeks

it felt like two years

I want to tell you so many things

but we complain about work instead

I feel my way around in the dark

searching for your boundaries

Oh!

there it is

I'll retreat to the safety of easy questions

how's work

how's your family

but I really want to ask

for all the juicy details

of your life with her

~

I GET IT NOW

I've made you the bad guy

for making me the bad guy

I AM THE BAD GUY

It's ok for you to feel angry

It's ok for you to feel sad

It's ok for you to need space

It's ok for you to miss me

&

It's ok for me to feel those things too

It's not ok for you to toy with me on purpose

&

It's not ok for me to push you when you're not ready

But I get it now

& that gives me

a new kind of hope

~

You're absolutely right
you're no one's second choice
you know your worth
the only one who didn't
know your worth
was me
does that make me
a bad person?
I had to leave
to realize how special
you are

Doubt
is complicated
is there room for doubt
did you give me any room
I was so scared
you didn't give me
any grace
maybe I didn't deserve it
(I probably didn't)

I guess you didn't love me enough

to find out

~

I didn't value myself

so how was I supposed to know

how to value you

~

What I did isn't ok

but would it be enough

to apologize

& realize

that I am more

than my mistakes

~

I realize the bar is low

when I have to say

"But I didn't cheat on you"

And yet

It's true

You never said

      "

      Hey Kell,

we're getting close again and I'd like to give us space to

figure out where we might go from here. I don't want us

to be seeing other people while we figure it out. What do

you think?

      "

You never said that

You—

      always so intent on communication

You never said anything

Why was this the one time

you expected me to read your mind

I never said

"

Hey,

we're getting close again, and it feels great, but I'm also scared. I'm so afraid of committing to you & getting hurt again. But it feels so good to be with you. I'm confused too, because I'm talking to this other guy & I really like him. I don't think I want to break it off with him. I don't want to hurt anyone, but I don't know what choice to make. Can we take a step back so I can figure it out?

"

I never said that

Me—

always so afraid of my own voice

I never said anything

Why didn't I step up

this one time

~

For a while there
all the tarot kept giving me was

Hanged Man
      Hanged Man
            Hanged Man

alright, alright
I get it guys
I need to leave things be
live in the discomfort
& let time clear the way
it's just so fucking hard
to walk away

~

I know you're still in love with me
it's why you're pushing me away
why you sent me a picture of you &
your new girlfriend
why you said you're too busy
to meet up for lunch

if you saw my smile again
you'd fall hard
if you heard me talk like a frat boy
you'd regret leaving me
if you heard my laugh
oh
forget it
your heart would be mine

you're afraid
you're so afraid
of loving me
of getting hurt
of being disloyal

I'm here to tell you that

it's ok

don't be afraid

love should make you

feel good

I've got you

I'm not afraid

not anymore

I can hold you up

this time

I'm stronger now

thanks to you

~

Do you still have therapy on

Wednesdays at 10 AM

I always think of you on

Wednesdays at 10 AM

~

want the pain

have the pain

hate the pain

lose the pain

miss the pain

~

If I were a bad person
I wouldn't care this much

~

tend to your heart

I tell myself

tend to your heart

pain accumulates

starts to weigh heavy

you need a structurally sound heart

to carry you the rest of your days

so take care

be tender

no one else will love you

the way you need to

love yourself

~

I like the pain

  heartbreak

  is a nice vacation

  from boredom

  I've never felt pain like that before

  in my life

  but I miss it

  some nights

  when I lay in your shirt

  & don't even feel

  the plunge in my gut

  I can smile and say

  oh, it's healed over

  but what's the fun in that

~

Someone break my heart again

so I have more

feelings

to write about

I should not have said that

~

Why'd you call me

just to tell me

goodbye

just to say

we can never be friends

What did you think would happen

when I started to cry

& asked you why

did you expect me to be chill

when you used the word

acquaintances

when you sounded so happy

talking about her

when you said you hadn't

thought about me in weeks

when you said

you deleted my number

What did you expect

I'm the one sending you emails at 3 AM

of course I'm not chill!

so why'd you do it

Intrusive Thought #1

If I kill myself now

I hope he feels guilty

for the rest of his goddamn life

Voice of Reason

1. You don't really want him to feel that way

2. You are the only one responsible for your actions

3. This pain will pass

  (I promise)

~

You have all the power here

You're doing to me

what I can't do to you

on pain of death

You know that

I know that

We both know

you're using that power

to make choices

you know will hurt me

That's a choice

~

Everyone says

I deserve better

than you

but what if

there's no one better

for me

than you

~

My therapist asked,

"Why do you let him treat you like that?"

Good question

It must be because

I believe that I deserve it

because

even though you're treating me

like I'm the scum in your shower

at least you're giving me attention

& that makes me feel alive

because

I like the pain

when I'm feeling pain

I'm feeling *something*

& that's better than nothing

So my therapist said,

"Maybe there's another way

to feel something"

She's right

But it wouldn't be the same

Expectations

I finally got an explanation

for why February was different than December

(in your mind)

You said,

"In February, there was no chance of us getting back

together"

(but in December there was)

So it's ok to fuck me & bail

when you wanted me purely for my body

??

The expectations were different

each time

I agree

The expectations *were* different

but that doesn't make it right

It still doesn't feel right

Don't you agree?

The expectations may have been different

but they were never exactly clear either

It isn't because we had sex
& you left for another girl
that I'm angry
I'm angry because
when you said it was a new beginning
I had an expectation

of what that would mean
Which you pulled out from under me
the very next day

You say you don't know how badly you hurt me
Take a look around
Let me show you

I didn't fuck you because I wanted to get back together
I fucked you because I wanted you to forgive me
I realize now how stupid it was
to give you my body
as a peace offering
& expect that this *new beginning*
would mean we would be friends

(was it stupid though?
or did you just fuck me over?)

I didn't realize how painful it would be
for my body to be used for sex
 & nothing else
You kept telling me he was keeping me around
just to have access to my body
but you are wrong
because what I had with him
NEVER felt
like what you did to me

You used me
in the purest sense of the word
(no emotional connection, remember?)
& that makes me feel worthless

The shameful part is
that I knew what was happening
I felt it
I hoped it wouldn't be so

but it was

I said yes

I wanted you too

Hey

I like sex

Sue me

I said yes

with clear expectations

But I didn't expect

to feel so naked

in the worst way

Can I trust

anything you say

Intrusive Thought #3

He doesn't want me anymore
so I'm going to choose
to be miserable & alone
forever
just to spite him

Voice of Reason

Come on man
Is this a joke
I mean
really

~

Do you think it doesn't hurt me

to think of you

every time I'm at the farm

& drive the Kubota past our shed

it hurts

every time we have family dinner

& you're not there

it hurts

every time I hear that song

"I Think We're Alone Now"

& remember us dancing

it hurts

every time I think of you

but it hurts less

every time

~

I judged you often & cruelly

I admit

My judgement kept me from loving you

the way I wanted to

The way you dressed

The things you said

The way you lived

was *you*

The full, beautiful version of you

One day I hope

to be me

with the same bravery

you were you

& I hope

to love myself

& maybe

find someone

who loves me too

Memories: #6

we got high on my family vacation

at the beach

played cards at the kitchen table

with all my siblings

after a day getting sunburnt

& windswept

we swallowed our gummies

& sat on the roof deck

bundled in a blanket

until you brought out

Taco Cat Goat Cheese Pizza

you slept in me and Amy's shared room

on an air mattress

on the floor

& the next day you told me

I embarrassed myself

in front of my family

high

at the kitchen table

we were sitting on the beach

when you said that

you were holding my hand

I felt so much shame

for being told

I was an embarrassment

for having fun

for laughing

for enjoying the goddamn

buffalo chicken dip

I almost cried

but didn't

at least

not until after you left

when I sat on the floor

in the rental house

& sobbed

until I gave myself a rash

Laura rubbed my back

& told me you were wrong

what you don't understand

is how hard it is for me

to let myself be free

& having you tell me

that the uninhibited version of me

was an embarrassment

to you

made me want to

suck myself back in

& shove it down

into the dark

where it came from

~

Is it possible

to love each other

without

being lovers

Left Right Center

I smoked weed for the first time

with you & your cousin

different family vacation

same beach

your cousin is weird

but he is kind

with frizzy hair & blue eyes

& a scrawny sense of self

he didn't make me feel stupid

for not knowing how to smoke

I don't think I got high

I was too afraid to inhale

but it was a formative experience

nonetheless

I wish I got to know your family better

your cousins

(blood & bonded)

& your sister

& all your crazy

aunts & uncles
I could have fallen in love
if only I'd had more time
to smoke some more joints
play some more games
drink some more alcohol
& bribe them all
with more peaches

~

Welcome to the now

(the only thing that matters)

you've turned all your beautiful love

into razor wire

held to my throat

threatened me

in the name of honesty

& your own vindication

does it make you feel powerful

to press that wire

to my throat

& watch me squirm

do you get off

on it

you must

because I can't think of a single reason

why you would turn all that beautiful love

into something ugly & cruel

& make me believe

that that's the way

it has to be

~

I know who I am

(who I was)

&

I hate myself

for it

~

This is me taking responsibility

I didn't respect your request for space
I own that
I slept with another guy
while you were under the impression
we would get back together
I own that
I asked for advice on how to keep the guy
you were jealous of
I own that
I took advantage of you
I was inconsiderate of your feelings
I treated you like someone who would love me forever
I own that

Your turn

~

My smile

melts

the iciest of hearts

you said so yourself

maybe it will melt yours

when I see you

again

~

You value me more than I value myself
but you've gone about showing me
in the shittiest way possible

Your actions prove to me my worthlessness
& your words obliterate my fragile sense of self

You've made me feel so much worse
when what you've really been trying to do
is make me see the truth of what I deserve

(I wish you were better at
articulating your thoughts)

Although
maybe I should thank you
because you've made me see
that I deserve to be treated better
than how you've treated me

~

I made a mistake

I reflected

I apologized

I validated

I'm learning

I'm growing

I've said & done all I can

I relinquish the control over you

that I wish I had

I've said & done all I can

There's nothing left to do

but wait for you

~

I have to forgive myself
I can't live with the constant
internal torture
It's killing me
I have to accept
that you may never forgive me
& let that be ok

I don't want to accept that
I want to fix it
I want a satisfying ending
But you're not a fictional character
I have written into existence
& life doesn't follow a narrative structure

I cannot move on
until I forgive myself
(I'm scared to move on)
But I have to move on
Otherwise
I won't be able to go on

~

You loved me so much

Big & Messy & Bright

I see that now

I see it all for what it was

But at the time

I wasn't ready for that much love to be directed at me

I didn't think I deserved it

I was afraid

I didn't how to

hold it

embrace it

accept it

Let alone

have the ability to give back

even half of what you deserved

"I'm sorry"

doesn't come close to what I want to say to you

I want to heal your wounds with my tears

& kiss the places where it hurts

I want to hold you & tell you

"I've got you"

& hope you know

what that means

~

we never

went to the Asian fusion restaurant you liked

we never

had sex while high

we never

watched *The Whale*

we never

saw the Christmas lights at Peddlers Village

we never

took a trip together

we never

did so many things

I wanted to do them all

I wanted to do it all

with you

~

Can I come over
      & can we cuddle
      & watch a movie
Can it not be weird

~

Stop taking everything so seriously!

    Literally

        It's fine!

~

We fucked each other up so badly

it's almost funny

we were both callous & cruel

but loved each other just the same

we both lost all self respect

& then realized we deserved better

we both learned how to walk away

but somehow came right back

we both had to take a good long look in the mirror

& ask

is this how I want to treat people

(at least, I did)

(I hope you did too)

we're learning the same lesson

from both perspectives

have you noticed that

we were both predator & prey

at different times

isn't it funny

that we taught each other these things

but we can't move past our pain

to see the possibilities that await us

~

You were lucky (unlucky) enough

to be my first love

A position I don't envy

or wish upon my worst enemy

I was an unrefined mess

in unfamiliar territory

It was hard for me

to learn the landscape of

love

Not only love

but

a Relationship

It was the most difficult challenge of my life

Harder still

to have the self awareness

to know I was fucking up

but not the skill to know how to stop

I wasn't perfect

We weren't perfect

I made mistakes

So did you

There were times I didn't treat you

the way I wanted to

There were time I didn't say

what I meant

There were times I tried to be brave

but choked instead

There were times I was mean

when I really just wanted a hug

I tried my best

(even if my best was shit)

I loved you so much

(even if it didn't seem like it)

You were my first love

& I think we did

the best we could

with the information we had

But we could always

do better

~

One day I'll be able to face you

with faded bruises

& a full heart

because I embraced the pain

kept it close through all these months

let it seep into my soul

& leak out through my tears

One day I'll be able to face you

with faded bruises

& a full heart

because I didn't turn the pain against you

I didn't make it all your fault

I didn't let it breed resentment

& a lifetime of anger

One day I'll be able to face you

with faded bruises

& a full heart

because I used the pain as power

many cycles of the moon spent on self reflection

many notebooks filled & ink spilled
making art from my humiliation & revelation

So that one day I can face you
baring my bruises proudly
& offering love from my full heart
without the slightest bit of self consciousness
because that's all I ever wanted
not to become bitter & jaded
but to become generous & soft

If you keep avoiding the pain
you won't be able to do the same

~

My favorite memory of us
(one I won't share)
only makes me smile now

I no longer cry
knowing we'll never have that again
I smile

~

I'd never had a boyfriend before
so, yeah
of course I made mistakes

I'd never broken up with a boyfriend before
so, yeah
of course I made mistakes

> I've never written a collection of poetry
> to process the feelings of a heartbreak before
> (& the love that came after)
> so, yeah
> this might be a mistake

(but I don't think it is)

~

Eclipse season

is doing me dirty

all the shadowy parts

of me

are being dragged into the light

honestly

it's hard to look

Self Explanation

So I'm reading this book called
Existential Psychotherapy
(just a bit of light reading)
& I think
I've figured it all out

This psychology textbook
from 1980
has made me see
everything you couldn't
show me

Existential Isolation
I am alone
You are alone
We are all alone

I used to feel secure
about my self imposed isolation
I felt safe
in my loneliness

That was a lie
I told myself
to avoid the immense fear
of being alone
being forgotten
being unknown

Until I had you
& became obsessed
with the idea
of being seen
of being part of something
of being loved

I used you
to affirm my own existence
I didn't know who I was
but you told me

The thing I'm most afraid of
is myself
& who I could become

if I embraced the freedom
of individuation

So I avoided that
scary little thing
by pretending
I didn't need it
because I had you

To live with the truth
of isolation
we need to
live with the work
of self identification

I need to build up
my stores
of personal worth
& identity
if I want to be the kind of person
who forms relationships
with people

because I love who they are

without the need for self validation

(and I really want to be that kind of person)

Of course

nothing is black & white

no one is perfect

or perfectly

self-actualized

I did love you

but you also served a function

perhaps the lines

got too blurred

One thing I know for sure

is that the strength of my identity

was weak

when we met

weak

when we loved

& weak

when we broke up

It's getting stronger
as I'm getting stronger
with every musty book I read
& therapy session I engage in
& new relationship I enter
I'm building the foundations
of my self
The self I need to be
alone or with someone else

I want a romantic relationship
with an individual
I want to be an individual
within a romantic relationship

I got a glimpse of that
with you
(no, not you)
you
      I want more

~

You don't know me anymore
but I want you to
I want you to meet the girl
you forced me to become
You're missing out

~

2/2

like

my smile

my snort

my lips

my laugh

my butt

my beauty

that's 2 more

than I ever expected

to like

any part of me

~

I'm wife material

bitch

get on board

~

I love love

when it's not me

who's in love

I'm so embarrassed

by my feelings

I grew up in a harsh world

where crying was prohibited

& you had to be careful

what you said to who

love was no exception

love & tears

have no place here

scratch that

there *was* love

just not the kind you say out loud

averted eyes

rush through the script

it's no wonder I don't know

how to show love

& I didn't know what to do

when presented with it

I'm sorry

I didn't know what to do

I'm still learning

~

I give just enough of me

so that you think I'm letting you in

but not enough to

actually let you in

I'm a master at

turning the conversation around

question before being questioned

talk about *this*

so I don't have to talk

about *that*

I'm an acrobat

twisting & sliding out

I am proud of my agility

but I am left with the

lack of connection

I was trying to fill

in the first place

never giving the full truth

for intimacy

balance

don't cry

in front of strangers

or maybe do

cry in front of those you love

cry in front of everyone!

be fucking unhinged!

just fucking cry

it's not cute

to be a bitch

but I look beautiful

with tear streaks

~

I like it when boys cry

They're not as scary when they're crying

Interlude #13

My imagination is wild. I'm not the kind of girl that stops checking out hot boys just because she's in a relationship with someone she loves very much. Maybe it's a consequence of being alone for so long. The yearning and the longing have been embedded from the start. So many books, read and wrote. It became my whole nature to dream. My livelihood and my survival.

Finding a real life man who loves me? Impossible. But it happened. It was surreal. An out of body experience. Accidental detachment. Dreams becoming reality was too overwhelming. Dreams were safer. Dreams *are* safer. So maybe I'll never find a lifelong partner. Wouldn't that bring too much anxiety? A lifetime of anxiety! There's already going to be a lifetime of anxiety. Do I need to add romantic anxiety on top of that?

My imagination was my identity. When I was in a relationship, my imagination disappeared. It was scared away by the tactile senses of reality. Reality was nice when reality was touching me. I wish reality touched me more.

I am afraid of losing myself in a relationship,

but who am I?

Will I ever know?

Do I choose creativity, but suffer through loneliness? Or

do I choose love, but struggle with freedom?

Can one really HAVE IT ALL?

~

The thing about life is

you have to keep taking care

of yourself

over & over

every single fucking day

until it's all over

I didn't sign up for that

get me out of here

~

Deprivation

Is a pretty word

Until you get a taste

Of the thing you've been

Deprived of

That's when

Deprivation turns to

d e s p e r a t i o n

~

I feel unhinged

Without connection

(extended edition)

I feel unhinged

Without connection

Unhinged meaning…

    Bored

    Restless

    Horny

    Boundless

    Desperate

    Devastated

    Lonely

Connection meaning…

    I want you

    To touch me

    To talk to me

    To connect with me

    To make me feel

        something

I want to feel something!

(other than unhinged)

(bonus track)

This whole poem is unhinged

~

Touch is tricky

I can touch myself

& be comforted

I can *touch* myself

& have a better time than you

could ever give me

but there's something about

your touch

your hands

on my body

skin to skin

is no joke

science & soul

I didn't know

what I didn't know

I didn't know

all I had to do was

reach out

& touch

~

when they touch me

I leave my body

dissociation   or   euphoria

I could go to rehab

for the addiction I have

Interlude #6

For the love of god, do NOT increase pressure if I get excited. Consistency is key! I know you like it when I squirm, but keep it together bro. It means you're doing a good job, so *keep doing a good job.*

~

Why are boys so fucking selfish

Until they say one nice thing

& I pledge my undying loyalty

girl

Get up off your knees

He knows what you can do for him

What can he do for you

Interlude #5

I want to give up. I want to lie still and let him fuck him. *Let him.* A particular choice of words, chosen to imply passive consent. It's not exactly that I don't want to have sex. It means I want to feel physically and emotionally fulfilled, but perhaps without any foreign objects being thrust into my vagina. But hey, if that's the only vehicle to achieve fulfillment, who am I to decline.

I don't like it when guys pull their penis almost completely out before thrusting all the way back in. It feels like I'm on a boat in choppy waters. Slightly seasick but perversely enjoying the drop in my stomach every time the boat bobs in the valley of a wave.

My body braces against instead of opens up to.

What happened to some good old fashioned grinding? There's a time and a place for the hard knocks, but some of us are just sad girls who would like a gentle rocking. Have a little compassion boys.

~

Call me Alexander Hamilton

cuz I'm never gonna be satisfied

~

I wonder what my future lovers are doing right now

Are they in love

Are they unhappy

Are they lonely

Are they going through a hard time

Are they having the best time

Are they in another time zone

Are they in therapy

Are they making mistakes

Are they working hard

Are they missing someone

Are they losing someone

Are they doing the best they can

Are they looking for me

~

I want a life

with someone

ya hear that Mom

I don't want to be alone forever!

I never thought this day would come

I'd like to thank the academy

& my parents

& my sisters

for putting up with my

cynicism & sadness

but mostly

I want to thank

You

for showing me

that being with someone

isn't a burden

but a privilege

~

Touch is
a portal
to a dimension
where everything is ok

Touch is
a trust fall

Touch is
your favorite song
on a shitty day

Touch is
connection

Touch is
hope

Touch is

a feeling

I would kill for

Touch is

a perfect line

in a perfect poem

Touch is

all I want

~

If Taylor Swift has taught me anything

it's that

you can be sad about your exes

and still

exit stage left

into the arms of your current lover

~

I just want to love you
I don't understand why you
won't accept my love

~

I need

a good cry

&

a good fuck

preferably both

fuck first

then cry

classic

1-2

punch

never fails

~

Am I delusional
or is this just how love
is supposed to feel

~

I know we weren't dating

& I wasn't your girlfriend

& we didn't break up

in the traditional sense

but I'm going to use those terms anyway

because it makes it easier

to write about

I hope you don't mind

or think I'm delusional

I mean, I am

but not about that

I know what we had

even if the words are hard to find

this is just a heads up

that I assigned

a little more structure

to our relationship

post mortem

hope that's ok

Apology Tour

To the boy who lived in 1204

Consider this my apology tour

If you've read everything thus far
& come away thinking

> well, fuck
>
> was she pining over her ex boyfriend the whole
>
> time we were together

Let me say

with complete honesty

the answer is

> no

The truth is

I met you way too soon

after I broke up with him

That's on me

If you've read everything thus far

you also know

I had no fucking clue

what I was doing

before/after/since

Yes,

I was working through the emotions of my breakup with

him

at the same time

I was with you

Yes,

I did keep that side of myself from you

but only because

I didn't want to give him the power

to taint what we had

Yes,

there were times I missed him

there were times I talked to him

there were times I fucked him

(which I told you about via unhinged voice memo that

winter day I had a cold)

(you said you didn't care)

        (maybe you don't care about any of this)

  (maybe I'm humiliating myself by caring more than you

                          do)

(but vulnerability is brave)
(and you told me I was brave)

It's hard to admit all that
& still say
I was kind of falling in love with you

Two opposing things can be true
at the same time
I know you have the emotional intelligence
to understand that

So even though I sometimes wish
I had met you
at a time when I was struggling
with less emotional weight
I also know
that this is how it was meant to happen
I wonder if you also wish
you had met me at a time
when you were struggling
with less emotional weight

We're both so guarded
but our inner worlds run deep
We were drowning
for very different reasons
& we never really talked about
those reasons
with each other

So this is me saying I'm sorry
for keeping my emotional landscape
a secret
It's not so secret anymore

I'd be lying if I said I wasn't scared
of hurting you
by revealing all my volatile feelings
about him
I'm scared
that you will hate me
after you read the truth
of my sadness
It would kill me

if you ever believed

I never cared about you

I cared about you

from the very beginning

From our first date at the diner

      my hounds tooth coat

      your French thrift store jacket

      we went to the park after

      to put off the inevitable goodbye

      I got blisters from my sister's Docs

      but it was worth it

      we stood in the parking lot talking

      & talking

      & talking

      about nothing

      I didn't want to say goodbye

I never wanted to say goodbye

You became more than a distraction

You became the destination

So I'm sorry I didn't tell you everything

I'm sorry I didn't let you in
I'm sorry that I pushed my way
into your world
when you tried to block the door
& I'm sorry I couldn't be brave
when I needed to be

You are exactly what I needed
when I needed it
You were brave
(frustrating as shit, but brave)

All this to say
I am good at hiding
but I'm no actress
All of my words
& all of my actions
came from a place of genuine
love & care
for you
& I hope you can accept me
& all my unhinged feelings

with the same genuine

love & care

you've always shown me

We joke about

how bad we are at communicating

our feelings

but this is me trying

To the boy who lived in 1204

Consider this my apology tour

Memories: #2

I dragged you to the beach

in winter

you're not from around here

are you

we walked

I said "is it weird that we don't have anything to talk
about?"

you said "no"

you have a nice profile

I noticed that your eyes are blue

we skipped on the sand

Playa Bowls was closed

I drove you home

the sun was setting

you put your hand on my thigh

you closed your eyes

in the passenger seat

I was scared

but I placed my hand over yours

I smiled

you fell asleep

I didn't know peace

like that

could be

for me

no

it's not weird at all

~

This is a new kind of love for me

there's so much space

I can walk around with my arms wide

& not run into you

it was scary at first

insecurity says

he doesn't care about you

he's bored by you

he doesn't want to spend time with you

insecurity can

suck my dick

truth says

he shows he cares in many ways

if he was bored he would leave

he enjoys the time he spends with you

yeah

we're both guarded

but we're both trying

space means

independence

freedom

not

reliance

dependence

space is exactly what I wanted

on paper

reality is hard

but I'm growing into all the room

you're giving me

Interlude #1

I want nothing more than to rub O.'s back as he tells me all his problems. I can't explain why I want this, except that I care about him and I want a distraction from the constant pain of being in my own brain.

Is this my cosmic intuition or am I just desperate? Why does desperation have a negative connotation? All it means is to have a strong desire for something. Strong desire doesn't feel like enough of what I feel in this situation.

I know I can't solve O.'s problems. I don't even want to try. But I want to know. His feelings are precious to me, which seems out of proportion to how well I know him. I suppose I'm destined to see people as wells of experience and inspiration. Something to mine for my own satisfaction. I don't like how nefarious that sounds. I want to help people. I want to help ease O.'s pain. I don't like to see him in pain. It hurts me too. O. is out of sight, but not out of mind. How will I survive life being attached to every person I let into my life?? People are supposed to come and go. But I'm not done with O. And I know he's not done with me. I can feel it.

But…what about what he wants? He feels he can't handle a close relationship right now. I understand that feeling so well. That's how I've felt my whole life.

I want to wrap my arms around his solid body. I want to peel back his layers one by one. I want to be given a chance to love him. I know I could do such a good job. I could make you happy, O. It'll hurt like hell when you have to leave, but this time I'm ready.

I'm ready to buy you tea and watch 80s movies every time you're sad. We can cuddle when you get home from long missions. I'll text you to be safe. You can send me stupid memes and I'll pretend they're funny. You wouldn't have to be alone.

I'm going to manifest the motherfucking shit out of our relationship. You won't regret fucking an astrology girlie. I can promise you that. All you have to do is accept it. Fucking text me back and be nice and spontaneous and ask me to come over. Be fucking brave! I'm ready.

~

When I said

how are you feeling

right now

you said

there's a hot girl

in my bed

& brownies in the oven

so I'm feeling great

~

I think my love language is
words of affirmation
cuz you keep saying nice things to me
& it makes me want to crawl into your lap
& live there forever

~

I'd known you almost two months

when you said you were sorry

but your life had become too stressful

& you didn't have space for me

you said

"I'm sorry things between us had to end this way"

     & I said

     NOPE

I'm not going anywhere

I do not accept your rejection

I pushed back

the bravest thing I've ever done

I just knew

in the golden threads of my core

it was not the end for us

I said that we could be friends

I said I was worried about you

I saw you isolating yourself

& I told you that you didn't need to do that

I told you there were people who cared about you

I cared about you

& I would be there for you

until the very end

You left me on read for a week

but you came back

I knew you'd come back

I'm so glad you came back

You've rejected me countless times

since then

But I always come back

I'm not ready to give up

on you

yet

~

You're so practical
I like the way you see things

You once said
you liked yourself because there was no other choice
I did a double take
is it really that simple

You once said
we're just two sad people figuring things out
I wrote it on a Posit-it note
I read it every day

You're so practical
it makes me feel crazy

You once said
my problem was that I read too many books
you're not wrong
my ideas of love are fucked
but you are wrong

because it's not a problem
to have feelings
I just wanted to talk to you
I just wanted to talk things through with you

You said
"I don't know where you're coming from
There's nothing we can do about it now"

I like the way you see things
but the way you see things
made it hard for you to understand
the way I see things

You're so practical
it makes me feel delusional

~

Remember when you said
"I'll text you more
as soon as I figure out how"
& I was like
what the fuck
& my sisters were like
what the fuck
& my friends were like
what the fuck
because I remember
& I can't stop laughing
what the fuck bro
you can do better than that

~

You haven't been outside today?
Come over immediately
I'm going to make you
touch a tree

~

When I start checking my phone
more often
& no one's there
I know I need some
social interaction
ain't nobody missing me
but I'm missing you

~

I give you my body

so I don't have to give you my brain

you can have all the

soft, warm, wet

parts of my flesh

they mean less to me

than the

soft, warm, wet

parts of my mind

~

every time I flirted with you
you left me on read

why

~

You don't enjoy texting…

so call me

write a letter

send a goddamn carrier pigeon

or

(god forbid)

invite me to hang out!

it's not about the texting

it's about the connection

fucking connect!

I'm starving for you

~

I feel anxious because I don't know when I'm going to see you next. You're busy during the week. Your parents are coming down to visit you this weekend and I'm gonna go out on a limb and assume I won't be invited to Sunday brunch. Which means I'll see you…when exactly? I don't want to be clingy. I don't want to be unreasonable. I'm not your girlfriend. I'm not a priority in your life. I have no right to your time and attention. All of that is very clear to me. But I want to see you as much as I can anyway. Is that ok with you?

--A text I never sent

~

You wanted me
No one has ever wanted me
the way that you did

It's hard to look you in the eye
In case you change your mind

Memories: #10

I spilled my tea

cuz you were touching me

two hours straight

that's what I call foreplay

baby

I'm slow to warm up

but you did it just right

you said

"is something distracting you?"

only the climax

of the slasher movie

we were watching

I missed the best part

cuz you almost

made me come

I can always watch the movie

again

but I'll never be in that

moment

again

my sweaty hand

over yours

cuz you were

touching me

& I was spilling

my tea

~

I loved the way you whispered in my ear
My favorite recurring phrase was
"I wish I could fuck you every day"

I always thought
Who the fuck is stopping you!
(not me)

Is that a thing you said
to make me feel desired
or
Did you actually desire
what you said

~

You texted

"Hey, you"

I smiled

I'm smiling now, writing this

Hey, you!

Hey, you

right back

~

I worry what will happen

when you leave

& I'm alone again

I won't be so happy

anymore

I've always been

not so happy

I didn't think it had anything to do with

being alone

I liked being alone

right?

the thing is

I didn't know

what being *not alone*

felt like

surprise!

I'm lonely as fuck

I have been for about

twenty years

is that all it was?

loneliness

huh

wish I'd figured that out sooner

~

You were surprised

After so many months

When I said I was uncomfortable

Receiving your full attention

Would you be surprised if I told you

No one has ever called me beautiful

No one but you

No one has ever claimed I was a giving person

No one but you

No one has ever praised me for being a wonderful

supporter

No one but you

The thing you never said was

I want

No one but you

~

I'm coming over later

Consider this my manifesto

I'm going to—

Take your hand

Lead you to your room

Say "sit down"

(On the bed)

I'll climb aboard

Wrap my legs around you

Now

For the critical moment

I'll take my shirt off

(Just do it girl!)

Make eye contact

Kiss you

I never kiss you first

I'm scared

I hope you're touching me

By this point

I know you like my butt

So that's a safe bet

Then I somehow

Have to take your shirt off

& stick my hands down your pants

Lay you down

Like you do to me

& then I plan to

Fuck your brains out

The end

…

…

Actually, no

I require cuddles

~

The hours tick by / bye…

Please text me back

Pleeeeeaase

I never wanted to be the girl who sits by her phone

Waiting

But here we are

~

The only time you texted me back
was when you were drunk
in a tent
halfway across the world

You were in the desert
I was in the snow

That shouldn't have been
the only time
you felt free
to text me back

Drunk
in a tent
halfway across the world

Memories: #3

you cooked steak & broccoli

I spit out the cartilage

I said "you write your paper. I'll sit on the couch"

you said "are you sure?"

absolutely

I watched you type

you press your lips together

when you concentrate

cross legged on the kitchen chair

then one knee popped up

I sit the same way when I'm writing too

you rubbed your face

asked me "why are you smiling?"

I said "nothing"

what I should've said was

"because I'm happy"

Sad Indie

coming from the kitchen

ceiling fan blowing soft

I would have fallen asleep

if I didn't want to be awake

every moment with you

you shut your laptop

you wanted to go to bed

I stood up

you hugged me

lifted me up

I said "I like being here"

you said "I like you being here"

I didn't want to go

but I did

~

I didn't know how heavy
the weight around your shoulders was
until I saw it lifted
that one day
you wouldn't stop talking
& your smile was different
I said
"you're so happy today"
and you said
"I used to be like this all the time"

You told me what changed you
& my heart cracked
into dusty little chips

The weight of the world
weighs heavy on you
but even your half watt smiles
brightens my day
even your anxious mind
is somewhere I want to be

I'm so lucky

to have witnessed

your full voltage joy

that one day

you wouldn't stop talking

& your smile was different

but

happiness is never a requirement

when you're with me

The weight of the world

weighs heavy on you

I see that

I see you

& I don't want

to look away

~

I would bundle you up
& take care of you forever
if you let me

I swear I'm not obsessed with you
(in a creepy way)

You know what I think
of you
You know what you mean
to me
(that's private correspondence)

So you know I'm not
a crazy girl
(relatively speaking)

But you should know
I would bundle you up
& take care of you forever
if you let me

~

I don't know how it feels to be you

but I'm no stranger

to depression

& the existential dread

of change

I'm no stranger

to the weighted sand

in your boots

& lack of lust

for conversation

give me the blood transfusion

of your sadness

I'm used to the lead

in my veins

I'd rather it be me than you

slogging through

the molasses coated world

I'd rather it be me than you

Memories: #8

we went to Chik-Fil-A

for milkshakes

because you wanted

something sweet

I'm always down

for something sweet

I curled up in the passenger seat

cold

like always

I was wearing pajama pants

the soft ones

you liked to touch

I played Taylor Swift

& when she said

"do the girls back home

touch you like I do"

I wondered what your answer was

at the drive-thru

they misheard you name

as John

so John bought me

my vanilla milkshake

thank you John!

sorry I left my half empty

cup

on your counter

when I left at 1 AM

sleepy

& no longer

down

for something sweet

~

I'm kind of a hippie
if you haven't caught on yet
I try to hide it
from people who I think
will laugh at me
but you won't laugh at me
will you?

You mentioned karma & fate
& I thought
alright,
maybe he's a little witchy too
but I never really showed that side
to you

But my hippie intuition
tells me
I met you for a reason
& I think you feel that too

The only thing

I still don't know
is if we're meant
for something deeper
than this
or
were you just
a passing lesson for me
& I to you

If so,
karma really is
a bitch
for showing me
the warmth
of what could be
then catapulting me
back into the dark ages

I don't like it here

But I'd rather fate
have given me you

even for a short time

then never at all

So I thank the sun

& the moon

& the planets

for leading me to you

when they did

& I thank *you*

for believing in karma & fate

enough

to let me believe too

~

If I'm such a meaningful person in your life

fucking act like it

~

When I get the—

I'd love to but can't

text

I'm reminded of my own desperation

Guess I shaved my legs for nothing

~

How humiliating would it be

if I asked you to hang out

& you rejected me

twice in a row

We're about to find out

~

When I said

> Do you want me to stop trying?

You said

> Yes

(but in a nice way)

I've been rejected by you so many times

it feels right

but

> Are you sure

is that you talking

or your depression

I don't like to see you sad

but I like being there

to hold you

> Are you eating
>
> Are you sleeping
>
> Are you laying in bed
>
> wishing I were there

I could be

I could be there

right now

All you have to do is

reach out

& ask

~

Looks like it's just
me and my vibrator
against the world

~

You were kind enough to say

that I deserved better

than what you could give me

that may be true

but you deserved everything

I gave to you

~

I hope you find a girl you love so deeply

that you ache to be apart from her

I hope you find a girl

you want to talk to all day long

I hope you find a girl

who makes you act like a lovestruck fool

who coaxes out your flirty side

who you call just to talk about your day with

I hope you find a girl you love so deeply

that you create a family together

& you all wear matching pajamas on Christmas

& bake banana bread on Sundays

& watch movies in bed with a big bowl of popcorn

I hope she loves you

the way you want to be loved

& she cares for you

the way I know you'll care for her

She's out there waiting for you

I can't wait for you to find her

1204

I miss your apartment

even though

the freezer door handle was broken

& the lightbulbs in the bathroom

were horror movie bright

& there was no peace

from the cars driving by

I miss your thrift store paintings

& your comfy couch

& your pinned map

& your cool patches

I miss your roommates

(Hey guys! Thank you for being so nice to me!)

I miss the sound my footsteps made

walking up the stairs to your door

I miss the smell of the stairwell

& the smell of your apartment

& the smell of your sheets

I miss your apartment

because it was a part of you

& I miss you

~

I wonder what we could've become
if you hadn't gotten orders to leave
the great state of New Jersey
(the jug handles really aren't that bad)

You said you would've wanted more
with me
& I wonder what that would have looked like
because I would've wanted to try it
for real
with you too

~

Maybe I should stop trying
to be friends with boys
I used to have sex with

They don't seem to know what to do
with themselves

Relax bro
It's not as hard
as you're making it

Memories: #9

you asked me

what made me anxious

about crowds

in the car

when we parked

no one had ever

cared enough

to ask before

you said

"we could go somewhere else"

& when I said I was fine

you asked if I was lying

and I said

"maybe"

but you didn't push it

you were a real champ

putting up with me

trailing behind you

like a scared little mouse

& in the crowded bakery

you rubbed my back

to reassure me

I'm sorry

that I was weird

& didn't appreciate

the kind gesture

it was

for you to take me there

(it really was so kind & thoughtful)

when we left

you said I was brave

which, yeah

kind of made me feel

like a child

but sometimes

you just need someone

to tell you that you're brave

when you do something

hard

so thank you

for seeing

how hard it was for me

& telling me

that I was brave

thank you

for taking me hiking

afterward

& listening to me

rant about

the benefits

of touching a tree

when you made that

sexual joke

on the stepping stones

across the creek

I was surprised

because you never talked

about the sex

we had

but the joke was funny

& I wish we talked about

it more

I hope you remembered

to take the dirty Chapstick

out of your pocket

before you washed

your jeans

your arms

turned me on

on the drive back

but you dropped me off

& went right home

we didn't get a chance

to touch

it was a weird day

I cried

when I got inside

because I needed to release

something

I would have sacrificed

all those memories

to have spent the day

cuddling

with you

instead

it was the thing we really needed

but never asked for

why didn't we ask?

~

I like to think

I cracked you open

just a little bit

it wasn't easy

but I'm proud of the work I did

& I'm proud of you

for a million little reasons

I'm so proud of you

~

The hottest thing you ever did

was cover my mouth

with your fingers

to keep me quiet

while your roommates

were out

getting Chipotle

& the front door

was liable

to open

any minute

Memories: #5

your car's leather seats

were cold

on my bare back

I never thought I'd

have sex in a car

I thought I was

too old

to fulfill my

teenage dream

but

you were kind

& took the lead

cradled my head

against the door handle

so I didn't get hurt

put your hands down my pants

I said "these jeans are too tight"

so you unbuttoned them

you said "I love holding your body"

or something like that

the windows fogged

I thought that just happened in movies

but it was real life!

sometimes

real life

is really fun

~

call me cutie   you think you can
one more time   call me cutie
& I'd be yours   & that'll make it all better
forever   because it will

I hate you for it
but please don't stop

~

I tried so hard
to keep us afloat
even when there was no *us*
to cling to

I gave you so much
of my energy

I put in the fucking work

I gave it all willingly
& I don't wish for any of it back

My only wish
is for you to try a little harder

Give me more
than the scraps of your attention

Put in some work

I know how you feel

so why aren't you trying

        why aren't you trying

~

All I wanted from you
was cuddles on Saturday afternoons

I didn't need to be entertained
I needed to be touched

I wish it hadn't taken me so long
to say that
I wish it hadn't taken so long
for us to connect
for us to be honest
about what we meant to each other

I wish we had told each other
what we needed
when we still had each other
within arm's reach

~

You're leaving in two months
we know this for sure
I'll be sad when you go
but something weird is happening inside
the lack of commitment
gives me the freedom to love you more
without the fear of
What Comes Next

It's been two weeks
since you've gone
I feel much more sad
than I had anticipated
I can pinpoint
the moment
you pulled back
to avoid attachment
&
the moment
I pushed harder
to avoid the pain

Constraint was freeing

but loss is a chain

tying me

to

What Could Have Been

~

I know what I meant to you

    my only question is

did you ever love me

    even for a split second there

did you love me

~

we never

watched *Karate Kid 3*

we never

had a sleepover

we never

had sex in my bed

I never took you

to my favorite ice cream place

you never got to

hold the lambs

you never even

met my sisters

I wish we had more time

we could have done so much

with more time

~

You'd be a good husband
I think
You'd remember to pick up milk
& always keep ice cream in the freezer
You'd pay the bills on time
& always look for the best prices
You'd carry the weight of a family
& rub her feet when she's pregnant

I wish for you
to share the burden
don't forget
she loves you too
she wants to hear what's in your heart
you don't have to be
such a manly man
you get cold too
sometimes

You'd be a good husband
I know

You'd bring her home to your parents

& drink tea together during the cold New York

Christmas

You'd show her your childhood

& invite her to be your future

You'd hold her hand in the car

& kiss her on the forehead in bed

I wish for you

to feel supported

& laugh a lot

with the one

you love

her smile

will guide you home

& you will be

her safety

~

You gave me:

a keychain from Nantucket

slippers from Germany

a hat from Maine

world traveler, you

All I gave you was:

candy

tea

flowers

because I live in central Jersey

& never leave

~

I think we could be good friends

if we tried

if we prioritized

friendship

over concerns of a more

physical nature

is halfway across the country

enough space

I know you said

that once you moved

you needed to move on

but call me

if you ever want to talk

I think we'd get along great

once we figured out

how to have a conversation

~

Your voice message
was the most beautiful gift
anyone has ever given me

Field Guide to Birds

did you panic

~

I was right there

in front of you

the whole time

you didn't take advantage

of what was

right in front of you

me

my love

my kindness

my body

my support

you didn't

take advantage

of my special offer

I hope you have regrets

~

When I miss you
I stick my face
into the hat you left behind
because I can still smell your sweat
trapped in the fabric of time

Is that embarrassing to admit?

Is it embarrassing to say
I miss you
& I savor your comforting scent
in the scraps you left me

If that's embarrassing to admit
so be it

If you could capture a fleeting piece of me
I'm sure you would too
even if you're too embarrassed to admit it

Memories: # 11

we were making out

on the couch

when your roommates got home

you said

you wanted a pastry

"let's go to the bakery"

you gave me the aux

the drive was only

three minutes

I wasted my opportunity

on indecision

you got a muffin

& a cappuccino

I got an M&M cookie

(thanks for paying btw)

on the drive back

I was prepared

I played

this song

called

"Just Fucking Let Me Love You"

it was a secret message

to your subconscious

just fucking

let me

love you!

we ate our goodies

standing up

in the kitchen

the cookie

was disappointing

but everything that happened

after

was not

~

Your texts all sound
like business emails
you don't want to send

I can't tell if you're trying to
get rid of me
or you want to be friends
but don't know how

I'd rather you be clear
than be polite

You're so hard to read
distant one day
gushing the next
You tried to push me away
I didn't go
only because
you said all those nice things to me

So I don't understand

why we can't be friends now
It doesn't have to be this complicated

I'll admit my mistake
if I am wrong
if I am delusional
& misreading the signs

It'll hurt if you tell me to leave
for good
but at least I'd know
where you stand

I think it's pretty clear
the ground I stand on
always has room
for you

~

My rose colored glasses

make everything look beautiful

& I love

beautiful things

~

Give me a minute to indulge
in my most glittery fantasies
tinged with cotton candy pink
worn through in the golden haze
between sleep & awake

I wake up next to you
you take me home
to meet your family
(I've heard so much about them)
they don't like me at first
I'm too timid
but I'll grow into them
I'm your date to your brother's wedding
then I'm your date
to everything
until our wedding
blue-eyed babies
open space
toothy grins
for years & years

I go there when it's quiet

reality a distant dream

meet me there sometime

won't you?

it's not so hard to get there

close your eyes

you'll see me waving

in the golden haze

between sleep & awake

~

I think you saw more of me
than I gave you credit for
I thought I was doing so well
at being a chill girl
I thought you were too aloof
to read between the lines

I underestimated you

When you said
"I think I see you differently
than you see yourself"
I was moved
by your observation

I underestimated you

You did see me
you just chose not to engage
with who I was

~

Thank you for crying in my arms

Thank you for falling asleep on my chest

Thank you for holding my hand in the car

Thank you for trusting me with your deepest pain

Thank you for buying me German chocolate

Thank you for letting me see you

~

I love that you drink tea

& black coffee

I love that you love to bake

& that you woke me up

to let me taste the brownie batter

I love that you

taught me how to play blackjack

when I came over in a rage

I love that you're an excellent student

(in all areas of life)

& an unwavering leader

I love how much

you love your family

& your job

I love that

you know how to make jam

& you were so proud of me

every time I cooked myself dinner

I love how thoughtful you are

at giving gifts

& I love when you

call me

cutie

I love that you love

candles

& dogs

I love your

weird sternum

& your soft hair

& the tattoo

on your

meaty forearm

I love the way

you see the world

I love how much of the world

you've seen

& the way it has affected you

I never said it to your face

but here & now

I'm saying

I love you

How do you guys feel about dating a writer?

Do you regret it yet?

~

I wrote these poems

in a two month

fever dream

of angst & uncertainty

hot sex & stilted conversations

longing for the dried petals

of the past

sobbing in the car

Amy held me

until I finally

sent those crumpled petals

to the wind

& found epiphany peace

everything became clear

when Mercury stationed direct

& my therapist said

I felt lighter

I learned

how to love

& I learned how

to love the pain

heartbreak is a bitch

but finding someone

who loves your laugh

is a drug

I'm a quiet girl

but I have so much to say

I have so much to say to

You

&

You

(thank you & I'm sorry)

I don't care

if you couldn't care less

(I mean, I do care

but vulnerability is brave

& I'm trying to be brave)

I'm telling you all of this

because I wanted you to know

& that's a good enough reason

for me

to finally

use my voice